y to

l report

ning

g Guides

Terry Loane

Published by the National Institute of Adult Continuing Education
(England and Wales)
21 De Montfort Street
Leicester LE1 7GE

Company registration no. 2603322
Charity registration no. 1002775

The National Institute of Adult Continuing Education (NIACE) is an independent charity
which promotes adult learning across England and Wales. Through its research,
development, publications, events, outreach and advocacy activity, NIACE works to
improve the quality and breadth of opportunities available for all adults so they can
benefit from learning throughout their lives.

**www.niace.org.uk**

For details of all our publications, visit http://shop.niace.org.uk

Follow NIACE on Twitter: @NIACEhq
@NIACEDC (Wales)
@NIACEbooks (Publications)

Cataloguing in Publications Data
A CIP record for this title is available from the British Library

978-1-86201-856-3 (Print)
978-1-86201-857-0 (PDF)
978-1-86201-858-7 (ePub)
978-1-86201-859-4 (Kindle)

All websites referenced in this book

# Contents

# Author's introductory notes

## How true are the vignettes?

All but one of the vignettes are closely based on real examples of teaching and learning that I have encountered, but with names and some other details changed in order to maintain anonymity. The exception is Vignette 2, which is an exercise in future-gazing.

## Use of language

To avoid the use of both awkward expressions like s/he and her/his and the ungrammatical 'they' as a singular pronoun, I have adopted a convention of using 'she' and 'her' when referring to those in the teaching role and 'he' and 'him' for those in the learning role. This convention is maintained within the vignettes, with all teachers being female and all learners male.

I have used the generic word 'teacher' throughout to refer to those working as teachers, tutors, lecturers, assessors, etc. Indeed my use of the word 'teacher' also encompasses those who may not think of themselves as professional educators at all but operate in some sort of supervisory, mentoring or supporting role. The only exception is that I occasionally use the word 'assessor' when referring specifically to activities that would be undertaken by somebody acting in this role in, say, an apprenticeship programme.

I have used the generic word 'learner' throughout to refer to those who may be described as learners, students, trainees, apprentices, candidates, etc. Occasionally I do use less generic words when writing about specific contexts (e.g. apprenticeships or higher education). I should add that I use the word 'learner' with some reluctance as its use can imply that human beings do not learn unless they are engaged in some sort of institutionalised or formal programme of learning. The reality is that human beings never stop learning – we are all and always 'learners'.

# What, no pictures?

If this book had been written, say, five years ago, it may have been necessary to include photographs or illustrations of the various gadgets needed to gather and manage evidence of learning: digital cameras, video cameras, voice recorders, memory sticks, etc. But today we simply do not need these different devices. Virtually every activity described in this book can be undertaken using a tablet computer, or using a combination of mobile phone and desktop/laptop computer. The hardware is becoming invisible – taken for granted. So I have felt no need to include pictures of hardware. The issue we face is not deciding which hardware to use, it is deciding how to use it most effectively.

# Chapter 1
# A revolution whose time has come

*Technology is available to develop either independence and learning or bureaucracy and teaching.*

Ivan Illich, 1971

## Vignette 1

Kim sits in her car outside the offices of Baker and Co. She has just spent an hour with one of their apprentices, Brian, for whom she is the assessor. She taps the screen of her mobile phone to access Brian's online portfolio. After she logs in, another couple of taps are all that is needed to upload the recording of the 'professional discussion' they have just had – which was recorded on the same mobile phone. She also uploads a short video that she made of Brian demonstrating his ability to fix a paper-jam in one of the office photocopiers. Now Kim calls up a list of criteria, and clicks each one that has been evidenced today by the recording and the video. She pours herself a cup of coffee from her flask as she thinks about the feedback she should give Brian. He has said that he prefers audio feedback rather than written feedback so Kim clicks the record function in the e-portfolio app on her mobile phone and says what she wishes to say to Brian.

Job done!

As Kim drives off to visit another apprentice she reflects on three things:

1. How much quicker and more convenient this whole process is than in the old days when she had to write up pages of notes after assessing a learner and then ensure that copies of these were sent to the apprentice, to the training provider and to her own filing system.

2. Because Brian is such a keen apprentice he may already have used his phone to log on to his e-portfolio and listen to the feedback – no longer are there potentially de-motivating delays waiting for paperwork to be delivered.

3. She left the house this morning without a pen, but it doesn't matter much – she hardly ever needs to use a pen these days at work!

---

## Vignette 2

Julia is applying for a job. She picks up her tablet and clicks into the ORLEA app (Online Record of Learning, Experience and Achievement). She adds the email address of her potential new employer and then ticks each of the items that she wishes the employer to be able to access: testimonials, a video of a presentation she made when she was a university student, a detailed record of some recent voluntary work, and details of a short dissertation she wrote last year as part of an online course. This is particularly relevant to the application she is making, and one of the great advantages of ORLEA is that it is possible for her to make the whole text of the dissertation available to the potential employer. Julia can choose what information she wants to put into ORLEA, and who can access any particular piece of information. A potential employer can choose how much of the detail he/she wants to access, as everything is hyperlinked from a single screen. Gone are the days of certificates, qualifications and degrees. ORLEA provides, in a convenient format, the actual tangible evidence of what an individual has learned, achieved and undertaken. So grades, exam marks and other forms of abbreviated evidence are no longer needed.

---

These two vignettes provide examples of a revolution whose time has come – the revolution in how we collect evidence of learning and how we make that evidence available to third parties. But there is an important difference between these two vignettes.

The first reflects the revolution that has already happened, during the last few years, in the assessment of what are called competence-based qualifications. Many assessors are already working in a similar way to Kim. This book will provide practical advice on how you can make the best use here and now of digital technology when gathering, storing and reporting evidence of learning.

The second vignette takes place in an imagined future, but not too many years hence, in which the revolution in how technology makes evidence of learning available has transformed the concepts and processes involved in qualifications, job applications, CVs, etc. As well as providing practical advice for the here and now, the book will, in the final chapter, look into what may happen in the near future. Much will surely change as a result of the enormous possibilities of digital online technology to reduce bureaucracy and to enable learners to achieve true independence in terms of what they learn and how they tell others about their learning.

# Chapter 2
# What do we mean by assessing?

*The best teachers constantly monitor what is happening to students as they set about learning and investigate when things do not proceed as planned or expected.*

Demos, 2005

What do we mean when we talk about 'assessing', 'assessment' or 'assessors'? Much has been written about this complex area, and writers love to stick various words before or after the word assessment to create a bewilderingly large number of different concepts and terms. An explanation of some of the most commonly used terms is given on page 8, but this is by no means a complete list. (If you're really interested in all this, try googling the following as well: ipsative assessment, dynamic assessment, criterion-referenced assessment, and norm-referenced assessment.)

One result of this proliferation of terms is that we can all too easily become unclear and confused about what exactly we mean when we talk about 'assessing', 'assessment' or 'assessors'.

In this book I will simplify matters by avoiding the problematic word 'assessment' altogether. Instead I will refer to two processes: assessing and reporting.

## Assessing

Assessing is a process which is an integral part of teaching and learning, and cannot be separated from teaching and learning. (Read Vignette 3 for an example of how assessing starts from the moment a teacher and learner first meet.) What I mean by assessing is broadly similar to the idea of 'assessment for learning', but I prefer to use the word 'assessing' rather than 'assessment' to emphasise that it is a process – or, more correctly, part of the process of teaching and learning – rather than a thing that can be separated from teaching and learning. It is, indeed, unfortunate that we tend to think of assessing as something separate from teaching and learning. This is partly perhaps because some of what is called 'assessment' is outsourced: we often rely on awarding/examining bodies to undertake this role, and within the world of work-based learning we talk of 'assessors' who are, at least in theory, not necessarily teachers. This takes our attention away from the important fact that assessing is part of all teaching and learning. What we can 'outsource' and separate to some extent from teaching and learning is the process of reporting.

## Reporting

It is clearly necessary to have systems for reporting to third parties on what a learner has done and can do. (None of us would want to undergo a surgical operation or an aeroplane journey unless we were confident that at some stage a competent authority had reported that the person in charge, the surgeon or pilot, was competent to undertake the job!) This reporting might take the form of a test result, a testimonial, an exam grade, a qualification or a portfolio. The process of reporting is separate from the process of assessing. And it is this process of reporting, rather than assessing itself, that is being utterly transformed by developments in digital and online technology – this is the focus of this book.

## Some commonly-used terms to describe different types of assessing

**Initial or diagnostic assessment** A process carried out at the beginning of a programme of learning to help to understand a learner's starting point.

**Formative assessment** A process carried out during a programme of learning to help determine how the programme should proceed, for example, by helping the teacher to know if more time needs to be spent revising a particular area of knowledge or if it is appropriate to move on.

**Summative assessment** A process that usually takes place at the end of a programme of learning as a gauge of a learner's success. It is the results of this process that are most likely to be reported to third parties as test scores, exam results, qualifications, etc.

**Assessment for learning** This refers to an approach that emphasises the importance of using the process of assessing to inform and improve ongoing teaching and learning rather than to report to third parties on success or failure.

**Self-assessment and peer assessment** This involves acknowledging that assessing does not always have to be carried out by the teacher. It can be very valuable for learners to assess their own learning and each other's learning.

**Synoptic assessment** This approach 'encourages students to combine elements of their learning from different parts of a programme and to show their accumulated knowledge and understanding of a topic or subject area' (QAA, 2006). The aim of synoptic assessment is to try to 'undo' the increasing modularisation and granularisation of the curriculum by adopting a more holistic approach to assessing what a learner can do.

To make matters more complicated, different people use these terms in slightly different ways, and the various concepts overlap anyway.

## Vignette 3

John is 63. He decides to take piano lessons again after what he describes as 'a short break of 43 years'. He finds a teacher, Simone, who has a fine reputation as both a performer and a teacher. Imagine the scene at the start of John's first lesson with Simone. He sits at the piano, raises his arms and begins to play. Simone has never heard John play the piano before and she knows virtually nothing about his playing apart from some assumptions based on the piece he has chosen to play (the first movement of a sonata by Mozart). Now, the instant John starts playing, Simone starts assessing. She assesses the sound he makes, how accurately he plays, she assesses how he copes with the more difficult sections of the piece, she assesses how he chooses to interpret the music. When John stops playing, Simone gives him feedback, explaining how he can improve and progress, and this soon turns into a conversation in which Simone acknowledges John's input even when he might disagree with Simone on some matter. Sometimes Simone plays and John listens. This process of listening, observing, conversing and making judgements is repeated throughout the lesson and in all future lessons. John has no desire ('at my age and at my stage' as he puts it) to take a piano exam or to perform at a high-profile concert, but he has every desire to continue with these stimulating lessons, which he feels are transforming his piano playing.

Two interesting things to note in this vignette are:

1. The process of assessing starts from the very first note John plays during the very first lesson. The process is almost continuous and is inseparable from the process of teaching and learning.

2. John has no need for Simone to gather any formal evidence of his learning nor to report to a third party on his learning. (Indeed if John did wish a third party to know how well he could play the piano he would do the obvious thing. He would simply let that person hear him playing – which is easier than ever in these days of mp3 files and portable devices with good-quality internal microphones.)

# Chapter 3
# Different types of evidence and how to gather it

*I should have liked to be asked to say what I knew. They always tried to ask what I did not know. When I would have willingly displayed my knowledge, they sought to expose my ignorance.*

Winston Churchill, 1930

In this chapter we will consider the different ways in which evidence of learning can be gathered, and how technology may be used in the process. More detailed information about using the various technology tools will be found in the next chapter. Many, but by no means all, of the examples are drawn from the work-based learning sector. This is partly because, ever since the introduction of NVQs in 1986, this sector has arguably been further ahead than others in its use of a wide range of techniques to gather, store and report different kinds of evidence of learning. But the techniques described are applicable across all sectors of learning and at every level.

## Objective tests

Objective tests consist of questions that have pre-determined correct answers. The most common example is probably the multiple choice question. Other types include true-false questions, multiple response,[1] ranking, and word searches. Such questions are ideally suited to being delivered using computer technology because:

- it is easy to create banks of questions and re-use them in different contexts;

- the software can mark the questions and with most systems can also provide different feedback depending on the answer given, thus saving the teacher a considerable amount of time marking tests and providing feedback;

- the software can be programmed to store a learner's score, thus providing an automated mark book;

[1] A multiple response question is similar to a multiple choice question except that there is more than one correct answer. So 'Which of the following is the capital city of England? (a) Birmingham (b) Paris (c) London (d) Leicester' is a multiple choice question, while 'Which of the following is a capital city? (a) Birmingham (b) Paris (c) London (d) Leicester' is a multiple response question.

- some systems support conditional branching (sometimes known as skip logic). This means that the questions presented to a learner depend on the answers the learner has given to earlier questions.

## How to use technology

All VLEs (virtual learning environments) have inbuilt tools for creating quizzes, and free-standing tools are also available, some of which are free of charge. Simply google 'quiz tools' for further information. Many of these tools are very sophisticated and will allow a teacher to:

- control how many times a learner is allowed to attempt each question;

- give a lower mark if a learner needs more than one attempt to get the correct answer;

- give feedback tailored to the answer selected by the learner.

Another approach to objective tests is to use classroom voting technology. Until recently this required rather expensive bespoke handheld devices, but there are now systems that can be used with mobile phones, making this approach potentially far more versatile.

## Hints and tips – Objective tests

- DO consider asking your learners not just to provide the answers but to provide the questions! I know an engineering lecturer who asks his students at the end of a particular course to work in groups to create questions for next year's class. He is not being lazy. He knows that proving that you can create questions provides far better evidence of deep learning than proving that you can supply the answers.

- DO consider using media other than just text in your questions. It is quite easy these days to include images and even sounds in multiple choice questions. Here are some examples:

    - 'Click here to listen to a short interview [in a foreign language]. Then select which of the following four options best describes the opinion of the interviewee.'

- 'Look at the five images of molecular structure and tick the image that shows a molecule of acetic acid.'

- 'Look at this map of Europe showing the borders of each country. Click on Romania.'

• DON'T make the mistake of thinking that multiple choice questions and other objective tests can provide evidence of all forms of learning. Human life and human learning is much more complex than ticking the right box, and that is why we need a range of different types of evidence. So read on…

# Evidence from things the learner has created

Constructionism is a learning theory based on the idea that people learn very effectively when they are engaged in creating real artefacts in the real world. (Constructionism is closely related to, but not to be confused with, the learning theory known as constructivism.) An artefact can be anything from a written document to a work of art, and almost all programmes of learning can involve the learner in creating things.

In work-based learning the term 'work products' is often used to refer to artefacts created by the learner. Here are some examples:

• a word-processed meeting agenda

• a written report

• a care plan

• a hairstyle

• the pipework of a central heating system

• a plastered wall.

And here are examples of artefacts created in non-vocational contexts:

- a piece of creative writing (either in the learner's first language or in a foreign language he is learning)

- a newsletter

- a chart created from data in a spreadsheet

- a painting

- a lemon meringue pie

- a musical composition or performance.

In almost all cases, such artefacts have some intrinsic value or usefulness, unlike, say, the answers to a multiple choice quiz. This is why creating artefacts is such a valuable aspect of learning. The artefact itself, or maybe a photo or video of it, can provide excellent evidence of learning, particularly if it is accompanied by proof of reflection on the process of creating it. This reflection could be in the form of a reflective account by the learner, a professional discussion between the learner and his teacher or a witness statement by the teacher or someone else closely involved in the process of creation. (See pages 18–22 for more information about professional discussions, reflective accounts and witness statements.)

## How to use technology

Art and design students have traditionally used a physical portfolio to contain examples of their work that they can share with peers, teachers and potential employers. (The word portfolio literally means 'carry sheets of paper'.) But digital technology means that the idea of a portfolio is not just limited to drawings on paper. We now have the e-portfolio (about which there will be more in Chapter 5) which can, through use of media such as digital photos, audio and video, contain evidence of almost any type of artefact.

## Hints and tips – Evidence from things the learner has created

- DO remember just how versatile this type of evidence can be. The bullet point lists of artefacts above are by no means exhaustive!

- DON'T forget the value of providing supporting evidence in the form of a reflective account, professional discussion and/or witness statement to clarify the context and circumstances in which the artefact was created.

## Observation

Direct observation is a long-established method of assessing the competence of a learner. It can be used in any situation where there is an element of 'performance' (in any sense of this word) by the learner. So observation can be used:

- for assessing work-related competence (the assessor observes the learner/trainee undertaking some aspect of the job);

- in music and dance education (in traditional music and dance exams the examiner is physically present and is in the role of an observer);

- for testing spoken language ability;

- for assessing sports performance.

A significant drawback of observation in the past is that it was not possible to provide a permanent record of the competence demonstrated during the observation. The only record was in the written notes of the observer/assessor/examiner. So moderation of the observer's conclusion was not possible, and this raised concerns that the subjectivity of the process meant that it was far from being reliable.[2] But technology now provides several ways in which we can keep a record of the observation, thus enabling observation to be used as a means of providing direct evidence of learning to a third party not present when the observation took place.

---

[2] The word reliable is here used in its statistical/scientific sense to refer to the extent to which the method used, in this case observation, can produce evidence that is consistent, accurate and repeatable.

## How to use technology

*1. Audio*

It has never been easier to make sound recordings. Virtually all modern mobile phones and tablet computers have internal microphones and audio recording software. Audio recordings are ideally suited to providing evidence in music, spoken language, etc. (For further information about using audio see Chapter 4, page 24.)

*2. Video*

This should be used when it is important to see what the learner is doing rather than just hear what he is doing. Until recently this would have involved the use of quite expensive equipment, but these days most phones and tablet computers incorporate video capability with quality more than good enough for what is required. (For further information about using video see Chapter 4, page 28.)

*3. Screen-recording*

If the activity being observed involves the learner using a computer, it is possible to make a video recording of what is happening on the computer screen while the learner interacts with the computer. This could be done while the assessor is sitting next to the learner observing his use of the computer, but it can also be done remotely with the observer in one location and the learner in another, using some form of screen-sharing application. (See Chapter 4, page 29 for further details about screen recording and screen sharing systems.)

# Hints and tips – Observation

- DO remember that using technology as outlined above means that you can now 'observe' a learner without being physically present at the time and place of the observation. Screen sharing and webinar software mean that observation can be done at a distance, but it is also possible to get the learner to arrange to record an observation session and then to share the video or audio file with the assessor for 'observation' at a later date. Read Vignette 4 for an example of how this can work. Remember, though, that you need to be confident that the session you are observing by audio or video is genuine.

- DO be aware of the so-called 'observer effect' – the fact that the behaviour of a learner might be affected when he knows he is being observed, particularly if an audio or video recording of the observation is being made. He may become nervous, and it is the observer's job to try to minimise this and to put him at his ease. Luckily, modern recording equipment is very unobtrusive. A learner is far less likely to be intimidated by a mobile phone or tablet lying on the desk in front of him than he would be by a large professional microphone on a microphone stand.

## Vignette 4

The year is 2006 and Gabrielle has been asked to support a group of trainee assessors and to assess their competence as part of a national project. The trainee assessors are located throughout the country. Gabrielle meets the trainees face to face only once, at an initial training session, but after that communication is by electronic means, using a VLE. So Gabrielle must do all the assessing remotely. This includes a requirement to observe each trainee assessor giving feedback to a learner. As it is not possible to do this observation face to face, each trainee is asked to make arrangements for a video recording of a session in which he provides feedback to a learner. The video file is then either uploaded to the VLE or sent by post to Gabrielle on a CD/DVD (this option being useful for trainees who cannot access a fast internet connection).

At the time this project took place (2006), the idea of doing 'video' observation was regarded as quite revolutionary, and all involved with the project were slightly apprehensive about how well it would succeed. But it was a huge success. This method of working is now much more widely accepted and the technology available today makes the whole process significantly easier. One concern expressed at the time was that the feedback session might in some way be 'faked' by the trainee. This problem was overcome by arranging for the trainee's manager to verify that the videoed session was genuine. But even if the session had been in some way 'staged' it would still have provided evidence that the trainee knew how to give effective feedback – actually it would have been much harder for the trainee to arrange a fake session than a genuine one!

# Professional discussion

Professional discussion has been defined as:

> a structured, planned and in-depth discussion recorded by the assessor. It allows the candidate to present evidence of competence and to demonstrate skills, knowledge and understanding through discussing the evidence and showing how it meets the requirements of the qualification. The assessor should guide the discussion by using open questioning, active listening and knowledge of the standards.

(OCR, 2013)

Professional discussion is a very effective means of assessing a learner's knowledge and competence, particularly if combined with observation. If a learner demonstrates through being observed what he can do and is then able to talk reflectively about what he has done and why he did it in the way he did, this can provide a powerful body of evidence of his competence and confidence.

One of the big advantages of the professional discussion is that it can be used as a means of gaining detailed and rigorous evidence of learning without the learner having to write anything down. This is important because many learners find it hard to express themselves in writing, and they may have had negative experiences in the past of written tests and exams. Indeed, most of us probably find it easier to talk about what we can do rather than to write about it.

Although the concept of the professional discussion comes from the world of work-related learning (specifically from NVQs and Apprenticeships) it can have much broader applications. For example, a conversation between teacher and learner could be a very good way of providing evidence of learning in non-accredited courses in a way that meets the requirements of RARPA (Recognising and Recording Progress and Achievement) and the CIF (Common Inspection Framework).

---

**Vignette 5**

Trishul is an agricultural apprentice. One day his assessor goes to his place of work and makes a video of Trishul preparing a field for planting a crop. After Trishul has finished the job he steps out of the tractor and, with the camera still rolling, he has a discussion with the assessor. They talk about why he has done the job in the way he has, how he would do it differently in different circumstances, the equipment he has used and various health and safety issues relating to this particular job. So a record of both the observation and the professional discussion is provided by a single video file, providing rich evidence of learning in a convenient and economical way.

---

## How to use technology

Although Vignette 5 provides an example of using video to record a professional discussion, it is more usual to make an audio recording. Audio is to be preferred in most situations because:

- it is easier to make a successful sound recording than a successful video;

- for recordings of equal length audio files are significantly smaller than video files, and so are easier to manage and upload;

- video adds very little to the strength of the evidence if it just shows a 'talking head'. Video only adds value if there is visual content that contributes to the strength of the evidence, for example if the learner is discussing something he has created, or if the professional discussion is closely linked with observation – as in Vignette 5.

## Hints and tips – Professional discussion

- DO remember that you do not have to be in the same place as the candidate to have a professional discussion. Skype and similar VoIP systems allow you to conduct a professional discussion over the Internet, and you can easily record the discussion using appropriate software. (For more information on VoIP see Chapter 4, pages 26–27.)

- DON'T make the mistake of adopting a 'one size fits all' approach to assessing. Although most learners in my experience would far rather talk about their work than write about it, there are some people who do prefer to write and who become quite anxious at the thought of having their voice recorded. (These are often the people described – in a very complimentary way – as introverts by Susan Cain (2012) in her excellent book *Quiet*.) If you have learners who find talking in front of a microphone really difficult, you may wish to use an alternative method for getting some evidence, for example through a written reflective account. Or you may like to take the opportunity to help the individual to unlearn his fear of having his voice recorded.

# Oral question and answer

Questions and answers do not always have to be written. Spoken questions and answers have the following advantages:

- Some learners have had negative experiences of tests and exams in the past and can feel anxious when facing written questions. They may be a lot more relaxed with a spoken question and answer session.

- Because the questions are not written down the whole process can be much more spontaneous and flexible. You could, for example, ask questions based on issues arising out of an observation or a professional discussion.

## How to use technology

For spoken questions and answers you can use the same methods described on pages 17–18 for professional discussion.

# Hints and tips – Question and answer

- DON'T worry too much when assessing vocational qualifications about the differences between 'professional discussion' and 'oral question and answer' as both involve a conversation between assessor and learner. I have known assessors get unnecessarily het up about the distinction between these, and I offer the following advice:

  - With question and answer it is the assessor who takes the initiative in the conversation since it is she who asks the question.

  - With a professional discussion the learner should take more of a leading role in the conversation, but the assessor should (in the words of the definition given on page 17) 'guide the discussion by using open questioning, active listening and knowledge of the standards'. When assessing I often find myself in the middle of a professional discussion saying things like 'That's fine, could we now move on and talk about XXX?'

  - When submitting evidence for vocational qualifications, one often has to state what 'method of assessment' has been used for a particular piece of evidence, but it would quite acceptable when submitting an audio file to refer to it as 'professional discussion/ oral question and answer'.

# Witness statements

It is standard practice in assessing vocational competence for an assessor to obtain evidence from a third party, often the learner's manager. However, many assessors have found it difficult to get written witness statements from managers in a timely way. So rather than send a manager an email asking for a written statement I nearly always arrange to make a recording of a verbal witness statement, in other words using the same approach as described earlier for a professional discussion. This can either be done face-to-face, or remotely, using VoIP. One great advantage of this approach is that it helps the assessor and manager to develop an ongoing relationship, and this relationship can be an important factor in determining the success of an apprenticeship or similar programme.

## Hints and tips – Witness statements

- DO provide the manager (or other witness) with fairly detailed information beforehand about the sort of evidence you are looking for and the criteria that the evidence needs to meet. Not only will this make the actual recording session more efficient and productive, but it is also a useful way of drawing the witness into a greater understanding of the programme of learning being undertaken. This is particularly important with apprenticeship programmes that are being managed by a training provider outside of the organisation employing the apprentice, as in this situation it is all too easy for the manager not to be involved closely enough in the process.

- DON'T make the mistake of thinking that the learner's line manager is the only person who can be asked to provide a witness statement. In some circumstances useful evidence can be obtained from a client of the learner's employer or from a peer. Clearly evidence from a workmate does not have the same authority as that from a manager, but peer evidence and peer assessing can be very good ways of encouraging collaborative learning.

## Log books and reflective accounts

Many programmes of learning require the learner to maintain some sort of ongoing log or journal. At its simplest this may be a detailed record of the learner's engagement in particular activities (e.g. the log books used by those training to be a mountain leader or a pilot). But learners can also be asked to create reflective records in which they describe, analyse and evaluate their experience. This could be a one-off reflective account relating to a single specific experience (e.g. a field trip) but more usually it would be in the form of a reflective journal written over an extended period of time, perhaps throughout a complete course. By providing both the opportunity and the incentive for learners to reflect on their experiences, accounts and journals can provide excellent evidence of deep learning.[3] A reflective log could be very useful in non-accredited programmes for providing evidence suitable for RARPA.

---

[3]Deep learning has been described as learning which 'involves the critical analysis of new ideas, linking them to already known concepts and principles, and leads to understanding and long-term retention of concepts so that they can be used for problem solving in unfamiliar contexts' (Higher Education Academy Engineering Subject Centre, 2011).

## How to use technology

Blogs are excellent tools to use for reflective journals for the following reasons:

- Blogging systems make it very easy for the learner to control exactly who can access the journal. A blog can be open to the whole world, shared only with a specific group, accessible only by the learner and a teacher, or completely private like a secret diary. (The last approach would, of course, be no good as a means of generating evidence of learning since a secret diary would, by definition, be incapable of providing evidence! But there may be situations in which it is appropriate to encourage learners to keep a private reflective account of their learning.)

- Blogging systems enable media other than print to be used. It is easy to include images, video and audio in a blog, and indeed one could dispense altogether with written text by using a podcasting system to create a series of spoken reflections on learning.

- It is much harder to lose an electronic journal than a paper-based one.

# Hints and tips – Log books and reflective accounts

- DO consider carefully how much 'scaffolding'/structure/support a learner will need in order to create a useful journal. Some advanced learners at higher education level may need little more guidance than an exhortation to 'describe, analyse and evaluate' their experience. But less-confident learners may find it helpful to reflect within a clear structure. I have seen good examples of apprentices being asked to keep a reflective log to show how they meet the PLTS (personal learning and thinking skills) requirements of the apprenticeship programme. Each of the six areas of the PLTS has its own section in the log with the criteria for that area listed. The learners are asked to write dated entries showing how they meet particular criteria within each of the areas, so there is a clear structure within which they build up their log.

- DO remember that a journal is not necessarily just about providing evidence of learning for third parties. It is also a useful tool for improving learning as it can provide a means for the learner to self-assess and reflect on how well he is doing.

# Chapter 4
# **The digital toolkit**

*Technology is best when it empowers the human input, enabling people to have more control over what they're doing.*

Maxwell Colonna Dashwood, 2014[4]

## Vignette 6

The year is 2009. Laura has been asked to lead workshops in e-assessment for several groups of trainee assessors in London. The focus of these workshops is the use of technology to capture and record evidence of learning by people undertaking NVQ qualifications. Each of the training sessions takes place at a different venue, and Laura has to bring all the equipment required with her to the venue. Her abiding memory of these training sessions is of carrying a huge suitcase full of equipment across London in the rush hour. The suitcase contained digital voice recorders, digital cameras, video cameras, 'Digimemo' digital clipboards, a set of classroom voting equipment, and a fourth generation iPod.

At the time of writing this, less than five years later, she would probably not need the suitcase. Most of the equipment in it is redundant, as mobile phones and tablets can now perform almost all of the functions that required separate devices back in 2009.

The world has indeed moved on in just five years.

As Vignette 6 suggests, today's digital toolkit for gathering evidence of learning may only contain a single piece of hardware – a tablet computer or a mobile phone. It would probably be quite possible to do just about everything described in this book using only a tablet or mobile phone. But our digital toolkit does not just consist of hardware. Software and 'apps' can also be thought of as tools. So in this chapter we will consider the various tools of the trade, both hardware and software, that are required for capturing evidence in various different formats: audio, video, still images, text, etc.

---

[4]Maxwell Colonna Dashwood is an award-winning barista, and in this quotation he was referring to coffee-making machines! But what he said about technology is equally true in the world of education and training.

However, before considering the contents of the toolkit, an important piece of advice: the toolkit is not just for the teacher; it can also be for the learner, and the more responsibility the learner can be given for gathering evidence of his learning the better, as this is likely to lead to greater motivation, engagement and responsibility.

## Audio

Virtually all tablet computers and modern mobile phones can be used to record sound. However, it is also still possible to purchase 'standalone' digital voice recorders. Prices for digital voice recorders start from below £20 so they are not prohibitively expensive, and using a standalone recorder may be a preferred option for some.

## Hints and tips – Purchasing a digital voice recorder

- DO check that the digital voice recorder you are thinking of buying records in mp3 format. Some cheaper recorders only record in wav or wma formats (or even a bespoke format) and these are not as useful. You may find that you need to convert the recorded audio file to mp3 in order to be able to store and access it in a virtual learning environment (VLE) or an e-portfolio system. To make matters more complicated, some recorders will *play* pre-recorded mp3 files but will not record in mp3 format. So you do need to read the technical specifications thoroughly or receive clear advice from a knowledgeable salesperson before purchase.

# Hints and tips – Making a recording

- DO make a quick test recording and check it before recording the evidence itself. When making a test recording, it is better to ask the person being recorded a real question rather than just asking him/her to 'say something' – which can result either in the person becoming tongue-tied or not speaking in a natural voice. I usually ask the learner what he had for breakfast that morning. Even if the answer is 'nothing at all' you will have captured a few words spoken in a normal conversational tone, which is all you need for a test.

- DO provide the following information, spoken by you or the learner, at the start of each sound file:
  - date
  - name of learner (or person providing evidence if it is a witness statement)
  - name of assessor
  - purpose of recording (e.g. title of qualification/course/unit)
  - 'part 1' or 'part 2', etc. if more than a single recording is being made on the same occasion
  - type of evidence being gathered (e.g. professional discussion, oral question and answer or witness statement)

- DO choose a reasonably quiet location for the recording but...

- ... DON'T worry too much about achieving perfect sound quality. The purpose of your recording is to provide evidence of learning, not a broadcast-quality interview. As long as what is said is clearly audible and comprehensible it does not matter if there is a little background noise or the odd unexpected interruption. If there is a disruptive interruption it is probably better to stop the recording and to restart after peace and quiet have been restored, giving a brief explanation at the start of the second recording as to why the first was terminated.

- DON'T make individual recordings too long. If what needs to be said in a single recording session is going to take more than about 15 minutes then it is better to stop after ten to 15 minutes and continue with a separate sound file. This has two advantages:

  1. It gives the learner (or witness) a 'breather' in which to gather his thoughts.

  2. It is far easier to manage two or three shorter audio files rather than a single long one: uploading smaller files to an e-portfolio is easier; and it is easier for someone moderating or verifying the evidence to check which criteria are met by which piece of evidence if they are dealing with shorter files.

## To edit or not to edit?

It is extremely easy to edit digital audio files using tools like Audacity (which is open-source software and therefore free of charge). Deleting words or sentences or changing the order in which information is presented can all be done with a few mouse clicks. But this raises an important question: should an audio file used as evidence of learning ever be edited? It is understandably tempting to delete any interruptions (e.g. a mobile phone ringing) which cause the flow of the talking to stop. It could also be tempting to delete a section of a professional conversation that shows the learner has a poor grasp of a particular concept. There is an ill-defined slippery slope between 'tidying up' a recording and, say, deleting the word 'not' from an incorrect answer to change the meaning, which would clearly be unethical and fraudulent.

The approach I have adopted in my assessing practice is never to edit a recording, regardless of what it may contain. I either use a complete unedited recording or (very occasionally) ditch the recording altogether if there has been some technical problem or the learner is having a really bad day and has simply not provided appropriate evidence of his learning.

## Remote recording using VoIP

The assessor does not have to be in the same location as the learner in order to have a professional discussion or an oral question and answer session. Voice over Internet Protocol (VoIP) systems enable us to have a telephone conversation over the internet and, importantly, to make a recording of that conversation as an audio file. The best known VoIP system is Skype, but other VoIP systems are available. If using Skype, the software to use for recording the call is known as Pamela.

It is important to bear in mind that the learner does not have to have a VoIP set-up, as Skype and some other systems permit calls to be made from a Skype-enabled computer to a regular phone number. There is a charge for connecting to a phone number in this way but rates are generally reasonable.

Remote recording can offer three advantages:

- The assessor does not have to travel to be with the learner and this can sometimes result in significant savings in time and cost.

- Learners are often very relaxed when talking on the phone in this way.

- Sometimes it can be very difficult for the assessor and learner to find a quiet place to make a recording in a busy work environment, and it is often easier for both to find a mutually convenient time when they can feel relatively relaxed, each in their own quiet environment, perhaps at home.

## Hints and tips – Using VoIP

- DO resist the temptation to have a video call if you are just making an audio recording. Using video makes more demands on the internet connection and this can result in poor quality sound or 'drop-outs' where the connection fails.

- DO check call rates beforehand if you intend to call a mobile or international number from a VoIP system. Call charges are generally quite reasonable these days, but you will want to avoid any nasty surprises!

# Video

It has never been easier or cheaper to create reasonably high-quality video recordings. Video is nevertheless a more difficult medium to work with than audio so should only be used when the moving image really adds value to the evidence. Video is the medium to use when the required evidence involves the learner being engaged in some sort of process or procedure.

## What equipment is needed?

A dedicated video camera, usually called a camcorder, can be bought these days for less than £100, but you may not need a camcorder as most still cameras, mobile phones and tablets can also be used to create video recordings. There is no point in buying dedicated video equipment if you already own a device that will do the job! Experiment with creating video on your mobile phone, tablet or still camera. If the quality is sufficiently good to provide the required evidence then you have no need for anything else. Remember that your aim is to get evidence of learning, not to make a blockbuster movie.

A problem sometimes encountered is that the image quality is good but not the sound quality. This may be because the microphone on the device you are using is just not close enough to whoever is doing the speaking. This can sometimes be overcome by using an external microphone, but the facility to use an external microphone is by no means universal and tends to be found only on more expensive camcorders. An alternative approach is to have a separate commentary, either as a separate audio file or added to the video using video editing software. Bear in mind, though, that adding a soundtrack in this way is rather time-consuming and requires some technical skill.

## Why is video more difficult to manage than audio?

There are several reasons why using video is more demanding:

- More can go wrong with video than with audio. For example, lighting levels may be problematic, particularly if you are making the recording in a dark environment or one with changing light levels.

- Video is more intrusive than audio. Not only can this result in the learner becoming nervous when he is being recorded, but privacy and confidentiality issues are much more likely to arise. (See Chapter 6, page 43 for more on this.)

- Video files tend to be much bigger than audio files so file transfer and uploading can be more difficult.

- There are many different formats for video files, and you are far more likely to encounter compatibility problems with different video formats than you are with audio.

## When is it appropriate to use video?

Because of the difficulties in managing video it is best to use it only when it really adds value and, as already stated, this is when you are seeking to get evidence of the learner's engagement in a procedure or process. Examples include situations where the learner:

- interacts with other people (but bear in mind that many such situations will not be appropriate for video evidence because to do so would breach confidentiality or privacy);

- demonstrates a craft technique such as creating a plumbing joint or decorating a cake;

- demonstrates the ability to perform a particular technique on a computer. This is often best done through video screen capture as described below.

## Screen capture

A very different approach to video evidence is to capture a recording of the learner interacting with a computer. This is called video screen capture and does not require any sort of camera. Instead it utilises software to make a real-time recording of what is happening on the computer screen. Video screen capture is a useful tool to use when you need evidence of a learner's skill in using a computer in a specific way; for example, using a particular type of software.

Broadly speaking there are three techniques that can be used for video screen capture:

- using software, for example Camstudio, which is a free download;

- using an online service, for example Screenr, which is also free;

- remotely, either using a VoIP system like Skype and recording a video call or using a recording facility within web conferencing software. The advantage of this approach is that a discussion could take place between the assessor and the learner in which the learner demonstrates particular techniques, and both the discussion and the demonstration are captured on the video file.

## Issues with file formats

Because of issues with file formats and 'codecs', video files can be problematic in terms of compatibility with different devices and platforms. (See page 32 for more information.) One solution to these difficulties is to use YouTube or a similar video-sharing website. Instead of uploading your video file to a VLE or e-portfolio you upload it to YouTube and then provide a link to the YouTube site from the portfolio. This two-stage process may sound awkward, but in practice a video hosted on YouTube will play readily on virtually any platform/device, while this is not always the case for locally stored video. Clearly you and your learners need to be aware of privacy and confidentiality issues when using a platform like YouTube, as most YouTube videos are accessible to all, but it is possible to make YouTube videos private so that only certain people with nominated email addresses can access them.

# Hints and tips – Video evidence

- DO keep videos short. A one- or two-minute video may be all that is needed to demonstrate that the learner can competently undertake a particular procedure.

- DON'T make the mistake of thinking that you have to do all the videoing yourself. In many situations it makes sense to get the learners themselves to create the video. It is so easy for them to use their mobile phones to make a really short video of some interaction or procedure when it occurs in a 'real' setting. Some e-portfolio systems make it easy for learners to upload video direct from their phone or laptop, and this can make life easier for all concerned. In some situations it may be appropriate to encourage learners to create videos of each other, and this can often be a valuable learning experience.

# Images

Still images are far easier to work with than video and no special equipment is needed. These days most phones and tablets will take photos of remarkably good quality. You would probably only need a dedicated still camera if the evidence required very close 'macro' photography; for example, if the learner was making jewellery.

Do bear in mind, though, that a single image rarely provides good evidence of learning. It is often better to provide a series of images showing different stages of a process, particularly if this is accompanied by a spoken or written account by the learner explaining what he has done, how he has done it and why he has done it in a particular way.

# Text

Much of this book is concerned with alternatives to text-based evidence. There are many situations in which spoken or visual evidence of learning is far better than text, and one of the benefits of digital technology is the way that it is now far easier to capture non-written evidence.

But there will still, of course, be many situations in which written evidence is required, particularly where the learning is of a more academic nature.

# Hints and tips – Text-based evidence

- DO, whenever possible, give the learner the choice between providing evidence as written text or in spoken form. Most people are better at talking about a subject rather than writing about it so this is often the best way to find out what they know or what they can do.

- DO try to avoid 'death by scanning'! Sometimes it may be appropriate to use handwritten documents as evidence of learning. These can, of course, be converted into electronic format using a scanner. This is fairly straightforward if you only have one or two handwritten documents to convert but it can be hugely time-consuming and tedious if there is a lot of handwritten evidence to scan. Technology should be used to make life easier for human beings, not more difficult, so one should resist being drawn into a situation where teacher or learner feels obliged to scan large numbers of paper documents. Alternatives to scanning include:

- taking a digital photograph of each of the documents, which is much quicker than scanning, but you will need a reasonably good-quality camera and a steady hand to get good enough pictures;

- simply storing the handwritten documents as hard copy in an appropriate place and including a reference to this within an electronic portfolio of evidence.

• DON'T make the mistake of thinking that all text-based evidence should be in the form of documents created using conventional word-processing software. This is appropriate for essays, dissertations, etc. or where learners need to prove their ability to use word-processing software effectively. But other formats, for example blogs and other social media tools, can be really useful for reflective writing. (See Chapter 3, page 22 for more on the use of blogs.)

## And finally, a few thoughts on files, file formats and uploading

Once evidence has been captured using a phone, tablet, camera or voice recorder, etc. the files containing the evidence must be stored safely. This usually involves uploading to a computer and/or an online system such as a VLE or e-portfolio. You need to understand a little about how files work in order to be able to upload different types of file with confidence.

## File formats

When information (text, images, sound, etc.) is turned into digital data it needs to be encoded according to agreed conventions. These conventions are known as file formats and you can usually tell what file format is used for a particular file by looking at the file extension, the three or four characters after the dot in the filename (e.g. .docx .jpg .pdf). See Table 1 for details of some common file formats.

VLEs and e-portfolios may only accept files that are in specific formats and these may be different from the formats used on the device on which you captured the data. So you sometimes need to convert files from one format to another. Very often you can do this using standard editing software (software used for word-processing and for editing images, sound and video). Conversion options are usually provided under either the 'save as…' or the 'export' commands. Other alternatives are to use file conversion websites like www.zamzar.com (which is free of charge) or to download file conversion software. The situation with video files is more complicated because as well as different file formats there are different 'codecs' within each format so it is doubly difficult to ensure that a video file is compatible with a particular device. This is why I recommended (on page 30) the use of video hosting sites like YouTube.

## File size

Working with very large files can be problematic because (a) they can be slow to upload, and (b) VLEs, e-portfolios and other file-sharing systems may stipulate a maximum file size for uploaded material that is smaller than the file you are trying to upload. The biggest files are likely to be video. Audio files and images can also be quite big, but the file size can be reduced by using 'compression', which means fitting more information into a smaller file size. There is generally a loss of quality when you compress a file, but often this is not significant in terms of the usefulness of the evidence. In practice text files are unlikely to be big enough to cause a problem. (All the text in this book can be saved in a file of about 200kb, whereas a single image from a digital camera would typically require a file ten times as big.)

# Hints and tips – Making large files smaller

- DO keep audio and video files as short as possible. Remember that two or more short files will be much easier to manage than one long file.

- DO think about 'compression'. Images can be compressed using image editing software. You should generally try to use the lowest file size that produces an image of sufficiently good quality to provide the required evidence of learning. See Table 1 for information about compression and audio file formats.

## Uploading files

There are many different ways of transferring files to a computer or online system from the device used to capture the evidence. The different methods are summarised below:

- *Use a physical connection.* Virtually all portable devices including mobile phones and tablets will have some means of connecting to a regular computer using a cable. This might involve the use of special software or a bespoke connector. A Google search is a good way of finding information that will help you to connect your particular device.

- *Wireless connection.* Bluetooth technology is the most common way to achieve this but wi-fi apps are becoming increasingly popular. My advice again is to use the internet to find information relevant to your particular device(s).

- *Mobile apps.* Many VLEs and e-portfolios now have apps that enable direct uploading of files from phones and tablets.

- *Email.* Sometimes the most straightforward method is to send an email to yourself from your phone or tablet with the required file as an attachment, then open the email on your regular computer and save the attachment. This can be very convenient as it is an 'any time, any place' solution.

*Table 1. Some common file formats*

| Type of file | Format/ file extension | Notes |
|---|---|---|
| Text-based | docx | The standard format used when creating word-processed documents using recent versions of Microsoft Office. |
| | doc | An older version of docx. |
| | odt | The format used for word-processed documents created in LibreOffice, OpenOffice and related open-source software. |
| | pdf | A very useful format for completed documents that do not require further editing. The advantage is that pdf documents are very versatile, being compatible with most devices. |
| | txt | The simplest of all formats for text-based documents. This format does not support the inclusion of tables, images or anything more than basic font and text formatting. |
| Image | jpeg/jpg | One of the most common formats for images. A big advantage of this format is that the degree of compression can be adjusted so that you can choose the optimum compromise between file compression and image quality. |
| | png | Another commonly used image format but not as useful for the purposes of evidence gathering as it uses 'lossless compression' and therefore tends to produce larger files than equivalent jpgs. |

| Type of file | Format/<br>file extension | Notes |
|---|---|---|
| Audio | wav | Very high quality, but very large files, therefore not much use in practice except for extremely short sound clips. |
| | mp3 | Probably the best known audio file format. It uses compression so an mp3 file is significantly smaller than an equivalent wav file. |
| | wma | A Microsoft format similar to mp3 in being compressed, but not as widely supported as mp3. |

Note:

1. This table includes some commonly used file formats, but it is not an exhaustive list. You may encounter other formats which may be incompatible with the VLE or e-portfolio system you are using. See the advice on file conversion on page 33.

2. This table does not include information on video file formats. The complexity of this topic and the way different 'containers' and 'codecs' operate places it outside the scope of this book.

# Chapter 5
# E-portfolios

*The biggest thing we can do is to work with staff to help them see that it's not about implementing e-portfolios in itself, it's about the way in which e-portfolios are used to support different aspects of the student learning experience.*

Jon Turner, 2012

A portfolio is simply a container, a case for carrying documents, drawings, etc. Likewise, an e-portfolio is, at its simplest, just a container for electronic documents. So the very simplest e-portfolio could be a memory stick or CD containing files that provide evidence of learning. But a memory stick would make a rather unsuitable e-portfolio, being an extremely insecure container. In practice, e-portfolios are online systems that contain features that add value over and above simply storing files.

It is not the purpose of this chapter to recommend any particular e-portfolio systems or products. E-portfolios and the features they offer are developing all the time so any recommendation could be out of date before you read it.

Instead this chapter will describe the important features of e-portfolio systems and the issues you need to consider before choosing a system. It is a big decision for an institution or department to choose an e-portfolio system. Training teachers, learners and administrative staff, and supporting them while they become familiar with an e-portfolio system are time-consuming and costly processes. So you should consider all options carefully as it is important to get the decision right first time.

## A taxonomy of e-portfolios

There are probably many different ways to categorise e-portfolio systems. Here I will divide them into three types, which I will call 'bespoke', 'open' and 'DIY'.

### 'Bespoke' e-portfolio systems

These are commercial tools that offer far more than simply being a container for evidence of learning. I refer to them as 'bespoke' because they are set up to be used with a specific range of criterion-based qualifications, and the standards/criteria for these qualification are built into the system. These systems are much used in further education and work-based learning (e.g. for apprenticeships). Such systems do not just provide e-portfolios but offer a complete management system for criterion-based qualifications. In fact it is important to realise that the adoption of such a system by an organisation will have profound implications for most of the management and administrative procedures associated with the programmes of learning for which it is to be used.

If you are considering choosing a bespoke e-portfolio system for a particular qualification or group of qualifications then you should visit the website of the relevant awarding body. The website will almost certainly provide lots of useful information, including details of:

- the awarding body's own 'in-house' e-portfolio system, if it has one;

- a list of e-portfolio systems approved by the awarding body;

- details of the awarding body's recommended or minimum specifications for an e-portfolio system.

## Pros and cons of 'bespoke' e-portfolio systems

- These systems offer far more than just e-portfolios; they are complete management systems which enable the organisation to track learner progress, manage quality assurance processes, etc.

- Most systems are customisable so that an organisation can modify to some extent how the system works in order to fit in with its own documentation and administrative processes (but it is only fair to point out that the organisation will probably also have to modify its own documentation and processes to fit in with the e-portfolio system!)

- These commercial systems are increasingly being made compatible with mobile phones, and their mobile 'apps' make it even more convenient for teachers and learners to access and work with the system.

- Bespoke systems are expensive – the adoption of such a system represents a significant financial investment for an institution.

- They require teachers, assessors and administrative staff to work in accordance with the procedures required by the system – there may be some resistance to this, especially among older and more experienced assessors.

## 'Open' e-portfolio systems

Unlike commercial bespoke products, what I have chosen to call 'open' e-portfolio systems are not tailored for use with a limited range of specific qualifications, but are designed to be used across a wide range of contexts by different types of provider. Many of these open systems are, as the name implies, based on open-source software, so they may be downloaded and used free of charge. For example, there are at least six different types of open and free e-portfolios that can be used with the open-source Moodle VLE. But some commercial products, for example Pebblepad, also fall within the 'open' category.

# Pros and cons of 'open' e-portfolio systems

- They entail significantly less cash outlay than bespoke systems and are therefore likely to appeal to smaller organisations and those offering less formal programmes of learning.

- They tend to be more adaptable by the individual organisation and individual user than bespoke systems.

- Although a system based on open-source software may appear to be free of charge, there will nevertheless be cost implications in implementing a system. It has to be hosted, either internally or through a hosting company, staff will need to be trained to use it and administrative procedures will need to change.

- Open systems do not have the same capabilities of streamlining administration in the way that bespoke systems can.

## 'DIY' e-portfolio systems

We need to remind ourselves that an e-portfolio does not need to be complex. At its simplest it can be little more than the digital equivalent of a suitcase. As Lorenzo and Ittelson (2005) put it:

*In the printed mode, as well as in today's electronic mode, students basically collected their work, selected examples to showcase, and reflected on what they learned.*

So all that is really needed for an online e-portfolio is a facility to:

- upload files

- securely control who can view what

- add reflective comments and feedback.

Most social media, file sharing and online storage systems provide this functionality, so they could be used as simple e-portfolios, and usually at little or no cost. Here are two short vignettes that describe ways in which DIY e-portfolios have been created using freely available online systems.

---

### Vignette 7

Martin is working towards gaining an ITQ qualification. The training provider with whom he has registered uses a task-book approach which requires Martin to undertake a range of exercises, many of which are closely related to his work. He first creates a blog using one of the many free-of-charge online blogging services available. He limits access to his blog to himself and his tutor/assessor. Over time he adds evidence generated by the task-book exercises to his blog, which thereby becomes a sort of e-portfolio. His assessor provides feedback through the comment facility within the blog. At the end of the programme of learning Martin writes a final blog entry confirming that the evidence in the blog is all his own work. The assessor adds a comment to the effect that the evidence has been assessed in accordance with the requirements of the qualification.

---

**Vignette 8**

David has been putting together a portfolio of evidence for a professional qualification. He saves all the evidence in a folder on his laptop. He uses Dropbox to share this folder with his professional mentor. The use of Dropbox also makes the folder available on his mobile phone and the desktop computer in his office, and he finds this really useful because it is so quick and easy to upload evidence that has been generated in the workplace.

When all the evidence is complete, the mentor collects it together as a single zip file, which is stored securely and sent to the professional body awarding the qualification, together with a statement of authenticity signed by both David and his mentor.

# Hints and tips – Choosing an e-portfolio system

- DON'T be tempted to make a quick decision! Implementing an e-portfolio system is a major decision for any organisation, and you need to avoid making a potentially costly and frustrating mistake.

- DO talk to as many as possible of your contacts in similar organisations who are using the e-portfolio system(s) you are considering adopting, and ask searching questions about the pros and cons that they have experienced.

- DO consider carefully the big picture when working out costs. The actual purchase/licence price of a commercial system does not tell the whole story. You also need to consider the time and cost involved in training teachers, administrative staff and learners in how to use the system. But on the positive side there may well be savings through implementing e-portfolios. These could include:
  - streamlining of administrative tasks (e.g. the system may automatically produce reports and statistics that previously required manual creation);
  - reduced reliance on paper-based storage;
  - reduction in travel costs for assessors as more of their work can be done remotely;
  - increased funding if the system leads to better retention and achievement rates.

# Two ongoing issues: Ownership and interoperability

If we think back again to the art and design student with his portfolio of work, there is little doubt as to who owns the contents of the portfolio. In most cases the contents clearly belong to the learner and can remain with him as he moves from school to college, to university or to employment.

But the situation with e-portfolios is not as straightforward. In practice, the control of the contents of the e-portfolio will often lie with the provider rather than the student. Especially with commercial bespoke e-portfolios the learner may lose any ability to access the evidence he has put into the portfolio once the programme of learning ceases or the relationship with the provider comes to an end. This seems both unfortunate and unfair. If we wish to encourage learners to value the artefacts they create as part of their learning, it is counterproductive to deny them later access to these artefacts or to require them to make separate arrangements for storing the evidence of their own learning.

One solution to this is to make the contents of the portfolio portable and to have agreed interoperability standards between e-portfolios so that material can easily be carried from one portfolio to another.

Further consideration of the complexities of ownership and interoperability is outside the scope of this book, but it is certainly an area to watch as future developments are likely. At the time of writing, the following initiatives appear to offer possibilities for further developments of interoperability and facilitation of learner-ownership of evidence of learning:

- Tin Can API

- Europortfolio

- Portfolio Commons (an extension of the open-source 'Mahara' e-portfolio system).

# Chapter 6
# Three important issues: confidentiality, authenticity and motivation

## Confidentiality

*All human beings have four lives: public, private, secret and online.*

Daniel Larsson, 2012

Society has understandably become increasingly concerned in recent years about the confidentiality of personal information held in databases. In the case of digital evidence of learning there are three classes of people for whom data confidentiality may be an issue:

- the subject of the evidence – the learner himself;

- third parties whose personal information might be used as part of the learner's evidence; for example, a care plan produced by a health care worker could provide useful evidence for a professional qualification, but there would clearly be confidentiality issues if the individual patient/client could be identified from the plan;

- organisations whose commercial confidentiality might be breached if sensitive information found its way into a portfolio of learner evidence.

Broadly speaking, breaches of data confidentiality fall into two categories:

1. Situations where authorised users are mistakenly given access to information that they should not be able to see (e.g. a non-anonymised care plan for a resident in a care home).

2. Situations where data is stored in an insecure environment, resulting in it becoming available to completely unauthorised users, including hackers.

Organisations need to ensure that they take steps to minimise both these risks.

Vignette 9 demonstrates just how easy it can be for personal and commercial confidentiality to be inadvertently breached.

## Vignette 9

Edward is a bookkeeper for a charitable organisation that receives much of its income in project funding for a range of projects. Edward's role requires him to prepare financial reports for the organisation. He is currently undertaking an IT qualification for which he needs to provide evidence that he can use spreadsheet software at an advanced level. He is a very keen learner and is proud of the fact that he has devised his own spreadsheet-based method for apportioning staff salaries between different projects. So when he is visited by Debbie, the assessor for the professional qualification, he wishes to share what he has created. With a click of the mouse Edward opens the spreadsheet and Debbie realises that the salaries of every member of the organisation's staff are displayed on the screen. She averts her eyes immediately and tells Edward to close the file. She knows most of the staff personally and feels it would be quite inappropriate, both professionally and personally, if she were to see how much each of them earns.

Debbie explains the situation to Edward and suggests a way forward. Before their next meeting he will prepare a copy of the spreadsheet with imaginary names and invented salaries. He can then go through this with Debbie, explaining his pride and joy: the formulae he has devised to apportion staff salaries to projects.

## Hints and tips – Confidentiality

- DO ensure that your organisation understands data protection legislation and operates in line with this legislation. A good starting point for finding out more is the website of the Information Commissioner's Office: http://ico.org.uk/ In particular you need to be aware of the physical location where online data is stored, especially if you are using a 'DIY e-portfolio', as there are specific legal considerations affecting personal data stored outside the European Economic Area, for example in online systems hosted in the USA.

- DO ensure that all staff are aware of the organisation's policies on data confidentiality and security, and have received appropriate training in this area.

- DO ensure that learners are aware of issues relating to confidentiality. In particular learners need to know the following:

  - What happens to their evidence and related data at the end of the programme of learning. Will the information be stored and for how long? Will they be able to access it for future use?

  - Who will be able to see the evidence, as this might have an effect on what they choose to include. For example, many apprenticeships require the learner to reflect on what happens at their place of work. Honest reflection might include concerns or criticisms of practices in the workplace, so a learner would need to know whether or not his manager had access to such evidence.

- DO remember that images and video can be particularly intrusive in terms of confidentiality and privacy. Although video is an excellent means of getting evidence of what a learner has done and can do, there are many situations in which using video would, for reasons of confidentiality, be quite inappropriate.

## Authenticity

One of the positive things about using digital technology as described in this book is that it enables us to broaden the range and type of evidence that we use. No longer are we limited to relying just on an individual's performance with pen and paper in the artificial setting of a written exam. But how can we be sure that evidence produced outside of an exam room is what it claims to be? How can we be sure that the evidence reflects authentic work actually produced by the learner himself?

Learners can sometimes, regrettably, engage in deliberately fraudulent activity, where they intentionally seek to pass someone else's work off as their own. Even more shocking is the fact that there have been occasions on which a teacher or assessor has colluded with a learner in 'cooking the evidence'. At the other end of the scale, though, it is all too easy for a learner to engage in inadvertent plagiarism if he is not aware of the academic conventions expected when incorporating material written by others in, for example, an essay.

Plagiarism is a problem that has, of course, increased as a result of digital technology because of the ease with which material can be copied and pasted from the internet. But technology also offers solutions to ensuring the authenticity of evidence. Two are described below

## Plagiarism detection software

This software can be used to check that essays and similar material are the original work of the person submitting it. The software can work by:

* checking submitted material against existing publications (as long as they are in electronic format);

* checking for collusion and copying between learners;

* checking for changes in writing style that could indicate that a passage has been copied from elsewhere.

But we should not make the mistake of thinking that technology alone can solve problems associated with plagiarism. As Jisc points out in a report on plagiarism detection:

> *Technology can only assist us, it will never replace the expertise of humans and... the answer to problems usually lies in process and procedures not technology alone. Electronic detection has its place in institutions but the real solutions lie in appropriate assessment mechanisms, supportive institutional culture, clear definitions of plagiarism and policies for dealing with it and adequate training for staff and students. If these areas are improved, the need, desire and appeal of plagiarism can be taken away for most students.*
>
> (Jisc, 2013a)

Actually it is not always necessary to use special software to detect plagiarism. In many cases it is possible, with all but the most advanced learners, for the teacher to be alerted to possible plagiarism by a change in writing style. Then it is an easy matter to copy and paste sections of the suspect text into a search engine to see if it originates in some online document.

## Triangulation

The term triangulation originally comes from map surveying, where it refers to the technique of determining the exact position of a point by looking at it from at least two different known points and carefully measuring angles. In education, and more generally in the social sciences, triangulation means looking at the same issue from at least two different viewpoints in order to be more sure of one's conclusions.

So if we use a mix of the different types of evidence described in Chapter 3 and a mix of the different technological tools described in Chapter 4, we are more likely to build up a true understanding of the experience and capability of an individual learner, and more likely to be sure that the evidence is an authentic representation of what the learner has done and can do. The ease with which digital technology enables us to provide many different types of evidence that can be put together to form a big picture is perhaps one of the best arguments for its use in managing evidence of learning. The combination of observation and professional discussion that is described in Vignette 5 (page 18) is a classic example of triangulation. By seeing the apprentice preparing the field for the crop and then hearing him talk about what he has done, we get an authentic picture of his competence. If further evidence of the authenticity of this picture were needed it could come from a witness statement from the manager.

## The painful death of the handwritten signature

One still occasionally finds people in authority (who should certainly know better by now) insisting that the authenticity of evidence needs to be validated by a handwritten signature. This is an outmoded delusion against which we should take a firm stand. Handwritten signatures are completely incompatible with the efficient use of electronic documentation. A scanned or copied version of a signed document proves nothing (as it would be so easy to copy and paste the signature from another source), so in order to use handwritten signatures for authentication purposes, organisations need to store and file hard copies of the signed documents. But the streamlining and greater efficiency that can result from the use of digital technology can be utterly compromised in situations where organisations adopt a 'mixed economy' approach, combining digital storage with large amounts of paper filing.

In any case, handwritten signatures have never been a particularly good method of authentication as they are relatively easy to forge. Digital technology provides far better means of authentication. For example, an email or discussion forum message includes a record of the sender's name and the time and date the message was sent. It is far harder to hack into an email system and send a message in someone else's name than it is to copy their signature, so we should have no worries about using such electronic messages as confirmation of authenticity. For several years I have used a simple exchange of messages at the end of an NVQ course to verify and authenticate the evidence. An example of the wording of these messages, which can be sent using either email, or the messaging system within a VLE or e-portfolio, is given in the box below. On no occasion in my experience has any awarding body had any objection to this method. It only seems to be funding bodies and their auditors who have a fetish for handwritten signatures. But in time surely even these slower learners will see the error of their outmoded ways!

---

## Example of authentication messages

From the assessor:

> I confirm that the evidence record sheets identified below are correct. I confirm that the candidate has demonstrated competence by satisfying all of the skills and knowledge criteria for each of these units, and that each unit has been assessed according to the requirements of the qualification.

> Unit 3A: 09 Dec 2010
> Unit 3B: 24 Jul 2011
> [etc.]

From the learner:

> I confirm that the evidence record sheets identified below are correct. I confirm that the evidence provided is the result of my own work.

> Unit 3A: 09 Dec 2010
> Unit 3B: 24 July 2011
> [etc.]

---

# Motivation

Successful learning can only take place when the learner feels motivated. So it is pertinent to ask what impact the use of digital technology as described in this book might have on the motivation of the learner.

On the positive side, the use of technology should in some circumstances help motivation by streamlining the process of gathering evidence and reducing some of the tedious work associated with traditional methods. For example, a majority of learners would far rather talk about what they have learned than write about it, so audio and video evidence can make life easier.

But, on the negative side, we have to consider the possible impact of the use of the technology on the quality of the relationship between the teacher and the learner, as this relationship can have a huge influence on motivation. The issue here is that some of the techniques for using technology could result in less direct contact between the learner and teacher. For example:

- evidence can be uploaded to the e-portfolio by the learner (and indeed by the teacher) without the need for any direct communication between them;

- the use of VoIP technology like Skype to make audio recordings of evidence can reduce the requirement for regular face-to-face contact, and indeed many cost-conscious providers see the use of electronic evidence as an opportunity to make savings in travel time and cost. This is probably particularly the case in the work-based learning sector where individual assessors often visit individual learners in their workplace.

Regular face-to-face contact makes it much easier for a good relationship between learner and teacher to develop naturally. So if the amount of face-to-face contact is reduced, the teacher must make more conscious efforts to develop good relationships and to spot early signs of de-motivation. The hints and tips box overleaf provides advice on how to do this.

## Hints and tips – Motivation

- DO make sure you keep in very regular contact with your learners even if you are not having frequent face-to-face meetings. In particular, it is very important to provide prompt feedback after a learner has submitted evidence.

- DO consider using audio feedback rather than written feedback. (You can do this using similar techniques to those described in Chapter 4 in relation to audio evidence.) There is some evidence from higher education (e.g. Gould and Day, 2012) that audio feedback can be both popular and effective, but the use of this technique is very new so there is limited research evidence at present.

- DO make a more conscious effort to praise learners, when appropriate. Informal encouragement and praise can often happen quite naturally in a face-to-face conversation, but sometimes require more deliberate effort in a telephone conversation or an email message.

- DO read the advice on motivating online learners in the January and February 2014 archives of the DawsonLoane blog at: http://dawsonloane.co.uk/blog/blog-2/

# Chapter 7
# Beyond the ticked box

*We cannot become what we need to be, by remaining what we are.*

Max DePree, 1989

This book has been about a revolution and how teachers, assessors and other learning professionals can work in a post-revolutionary world. Happily the revolution that digital technology has brought about in how we manage evidence of learning has, at least so far, been a relatively peaceful one. As Vignette 1 (page 4) implies, teachers and assessors are adapting remarkably quickly to the possibilities of the post-revolutionary world of digital evidence of learning.

But it is clear that the revolution is continuing. Some might say it has only just begun. So this final chapter will consider what may be coming next and how learning professionals can prepare for this and adapt ways of working.

The previous chapters of this book have described how technology can be used to manage evidence largely within existing qualification and accreditation frameworks (with many of the examples drawn from the world of work-based learning). But the new possibilities of digital technology are causing many to question existing qualification and accreditation frameworks and to ask if we can design better systems for managing evidence of learning. This has given rise to a number of quite radical new approaches, and four of these will now be described.

## Four examples of post-revolutionary frameworks for evidence of learning

### HEAR

*The Higher Education Achievement Report (HEAR) is designed to encourage a more sophisticated approach to recording student achievement, which acknowledges fully the range of opportunities that higher education institutions in the UK offer to their students. In 2013, 88,743 HEARs were issued to students (from across 27 institutions).*

(HEAR, 2014)

HEAR utilises the possibilities of digital technology to provide far more information about a graduate's achievements and abilities than a simplistic degree classification. It consists of an electronic document that includes a high level of detail about a student's academic achievements as well as a record of other activities and roles that the student has undertaken as an undergraduate. It has even been suggested by some that HEAR represents a first step towards abolishing degree classification altogether.

Bob Burgess, Vice-Chancellor of the University of Leicester and chair of the HEAR Steering Group, says of the initiative:

> *For employers, it offers the chance to see in more detail what students have achieved at university and make comparisons between job applicants. We hope that the introduction of the HEAR, eventually by the whole higher education sector, will mean that... graduates from university... will have far more to show for their academic experience than a simple degree grade or grade point average.*

> (Burgess, 2012)

## Arts Award

> *Young people... plan their work with an adviser, and keep a record by creating their own Arts Award portfolio. Young people can pick their own style of portfolio – this could be a diary, video, website blog – or something different altogether.*

> (Arts Award, undated [1])

Arts Award is designed for children and young people up to the age of 25. It provides acknowledgement and accreditation for their involvements in arts activity. Although clearly very different from HEAR, it is similar in that it aims to avoid the narrowness of conventional accreditation and reporting of learning. This is made clear by Trinity College, the organisation that manages Arts Award:

> *Each path can take a different direction... Whichever route they choose to follow, young people are always in the driving seat.*

> (Trinity College London, 2014)

## WikiQuals

*WikiQuals [is] based on a 'show and tell' process derived from medieval guilds, using the WikiQuals website to show to the world what WikiQuals students have achieved. It will be an 'open' and transparent model where learning will be negotiated and agreed, discussed, re-negotiated, shared and built upon.*

(Garnett, 2011a)

WikiQuals provides a framework in which individuals can research at postgraduate level in a self-organised context rather than through a programme provided by a higher education institution. Participants mutually support each other and are expected to find opportunities to self-publish their work, using online media as appropriate.

## Mozilla Open Badges

*Get recognition for learning that happens anywhere. Then share it on the places that matter.*

(Mozilla Open Badges, undated)

Mozilla's Open Badges initiative allows any organisation to set itself up to issue digital 'badges' that a learner can then use to prove that he has met certain criteria specified by the issuing organisation. Because the system is based on an open standard the individual can combine badges from different issuers into an online 'backpack', which becomes a portfolio of evidence of their learning and achievement. The system has not yet gained wide currency in the UK at the time of writing, but Borders College in Scotland has been using Mozilla Open Badges as a means for students to

*gain recognition for aspects of their learning that would not traditionally have been rewarded or recognised in a formalised way.*

(JISC, 2013b)

So this is very similar to the way in which HEAR is being used in higher education. In an article that is by no means uncritical of Open Badges, Ravet (2013) nevertheless sees great potential for this initiative:

*Open Badges have much more to offer than improving or enhancing what we are used to. They can provide the means to transform how learning is recognised and organised, moving the locus of power from the institution to the individual and the community. This will not happen by itself. Open Badges are no magic wand or lamp.*

## What we can learn from these four examples

HEAR, Arts Award, WikiQuals and Mozilla Open Badge are all very different in the way that they provide evidence of learning and achievement, but they have three important things in common in terms of how and why they have been developed:

- All four have been made possible as a result of developments in digital and online technology.

- Each in its own way has arisen out of dissatisfaction with the limitations and narrowness of existing conventional methods of accrediting and reporting learning and achievement.

- Each provides a greater sense of ownership for the individual learner of the processes of planning and recording her/his learning. The Arts Award website uses the catch-phrase 'Do what inspires you. It's your Arts Award' (Arts Award, undated (2)). But encouraging individuals to 'do what inspires them' and then to accredit the results of this inspiration is surely what lies behind all four of the initiatives.

The four examples of new forms of managing evidence show us how the use of technology can help address three problems inherent in conventional approaches:

- abbreviation of the evidence

- dehumanisation of learning

- reductionism – the curse of the ticked box.

# We no longer need to abbreviate the evidence

---

**Vignette 10**

John obtained a university degree in music several decades ago. On his CV he is entitled to write 'B. Mus (Hons.)' followed (if he so wishes) by 'Lower Second-Class Honours' or '2.ii'. But what does this tell us about John? Very little, other than that at some point in his life he passed a particular, yet unspecified, set of exams. We do not even know the details of the exams he took, and it would be very difficult to find out from the university after so long what the syllabus consisted of all those decades ago. Would it not be far more useful to anyone (like a potential employer) who had an interest in what John has studied and what he can do to be given access to more direct evidence? These days it would be extremely easy to use digital technology to provide evidence that might include:

- recordings of John playing the piano;

- a recording of an orchestral piece he composed in his final year as a student and which was performed by a student orchestra;

- a copy of the dissertation he wrote on early fifteenth century French chansons, together with his tutor's comments on the dissertation;

- recordings and programme notes for various concerts he organised and performed in as a student.

---

Virtually all traditional methods of reporting and accrediting an individual's learning have consisted of some sort of contraction or abbreviation of the evidence. Everything from '63%, could do better' on a primary school end-of-term report to 'MA in online and distance education, awarded with distinction' is an attempt to sum up the complexity of an individual's learning, skills and knowledge in a highly abbreviated form. Now this process of abbreviation was understandably necessary before digital technology was developed because it would have been impossible, in practice, to provide evidence from what historians call 'primary sources'. In most cases it would have been quite impracticable to provide prospective employers, proud parents and other interested parties with direct access to the actual evidence of an individual's learning and achievement. (It is interesting, though, that art and design students have, as mentioned in Chapter 3, always provided direct evidence of what they have done and what they can do through their portfolios.)

All four examples, however, provide direct access to much more transparent and comprehensive evidence of learning and achievement. They represent far less abbreviated forms of reporting. HEAR provides far more comprehensive information about the broad range of activities an undergraduate has engaged in. Arts Award involves the production of a portfolio of student achievements in any appropriate medium. WikiQuals encourages self-publication using electronic media, and with Open Badges, the criteria upon which the badge is awarded are encapsulated within metadata in the electronic badge itself.

# Technology can rehumanise learning

There is an increasing perception that the education and training environment is becoming dehumanised. We are losing sight of the whole person as we focus on grades, test results and tick-box lists of competencies.

Some feel that digital technology has contributed to this dehumanisation because it enables and indeed encourages us to gather and process huge amounts of data, without always questioning the value of that data. But the four examples in this chapter show how digital technology also has the potential to rehumanise learning, to place the individual learner and the complexity of their capabilities and achievements at the centre of the process. HEAR encourages undergraduates to engage in a wide range of activities and responsibilities outside of the set curriculum because these will be acknowledged in their report. Arts Award takes as its very starting point the unique interests of the individual and allows him to create a portfolio in any medium and format that suits these interests. WikiQuals provides a non-institutionalised framework of support for individuals to research a topic of their own choosing. (Fred Garnett, the founder of WikiQuals, encourages participants to try to 'solve the problem that annoys you most' [Garnett, 2011b].) And the Open Badges system has the potential to enable individuals to build up a portfolio of awards by selecting what suits them from a huge range offered by many different badge issuers.

# Human learning is greater than the sum of its parts

One particular form of dehumanisation is reductionism, the false belief that we can understand a complex system such as human learning by reducing it to its smallest components and seeking to understand each component.[5] This is what has given rise to the 'tick-box' culture in education and training, the attempt to 'narrow the multiplicity of human experience and need into a limited set of answers' (Sica, 2013).

But over the last 70 years scientists have increasingly come to realise that complex systems cannot be understood by looking just at minutiae. A complex system is, in a literal and scientific sense, greater than the sum of its parts, so we have to focus on the bigger picture and move away from tick boxes if we are to understand real human learning.

With the arguable exception of Open Badges, this is very much what the four examples in this chapter encourage. HEAR, Arts Award and WikiQuals all move away from an approach based on pre-defined criteria towards 'post hoc' acknowledgement of what a learner has done and can do.[6]

# What we should do as practitioners

We cannot know if any of the four examples described in this chapter (HEAR, Arts Award, WikiQuals and Open Badges) will prove to be successful in the longer term. But what we do know is that the techniques described in this book for using technology have the power to transform and disrupt traditional ways of gathering, storing and reporting evidence of learning. Technology has the power to rid the world of conventional mechanistic and reductionist approaches to assessing learning and traditional abbreviated forms of reporting. Technology has the power to provide far

---

[5] For several centuries scientists regarded the universe and the various systems within it as machines. Take the machine apart, understand each component and you then understand the whole machine. In educational terms this translates as: take a programme of learning apart, test learners on each component of the programme and you will then understand what learning has taken place. But over the last 70 years (commencing with the publication in 1945 of Ludwig von Bertalanffy's *Zu einer allgemeinen Systemlehre*) scientists have increasingly come to realise that we cannot understand complex systems by reducing them to the sum of their parts. We cannot understand human learning by reducing it to a series of ticked boxes. To be truly scientific in the 21st century we have to look at the big picture rather than the minutiae.

[6] 'Post hoc analysis' involves an acceptance that what is important in learning (and in other areas) can often only be determined after the event. It cannot be specified by pre-existing criteria.

richer means of assessing learning and of managing evidence of learning, and we should keep our hearts and minds open to new approaches that can enhance both teaching and learning.

I will finish with a slight adaptation of the quotation from Ravet about Open Badges on page 53. Ravet's message is an important one and applies not just to Open Badges but to everything described in this book. So here it is again, with 'digital technology' replacing 'Open Badges' and with the inclusion at the end of one additional, and rather provocative, sentence from Ravet:

> *Digital technology has much more to offer than improving or enhancing what we are used to. It can provide the means to transform how learning is recognised and organised, moving the locus of power from the institution to the individual and the community. This will not happen by itself. Digital technology is no magic wand or lamp. It will take time and effort to unweave the threads of rewards and incentives smothering innovation and free will.*
>
> (based on Ravet, 2013)

# Glossary

Explanations of terms and abbreviations used in this publication

**CIF**

The *Common Inspection Framework for Further Education and Skills 2012*. The framework within which Ofsted inspectors work when inspecting adult learning and other provision within the further education and skills sector.

**EEA**

*European Economic Area*. This includes the countries within the European Union (EU) as well as three non-member countries: Iceland, Liechtenstein and Norway.

**Granularisation**

This is the division of a programme of learning or a set of learning resources into separate small units, each of which is more or less self-contained and complete in itself. This makes it easier to re-use each unit in a different context.

**Jisc**

Formerly known as the *Joint Informations Systems Committee.* A public body that supports the use of digital technology in post-16 and higher education.

**NVQ**

*National Vocational Qualification*. NVQs still exist at the time of writing but the use of the term is being phased out as new qualifications within the QCF (Qualifications and Credits Framework) become embedded.

**ORLEA**

*Online Record of Learning, Experience and Achievement.* NB: ORLEA does not exist. It was invented purely for the purposes of Vignette 2!

**PLTS**

*Personal Learning and Thinking Skills*, defined as 'a framework for describing the qualities and skills needed for success in learning and life'. These skills are divided into six areas, each of which has between five and seven criteria.

**RARPA**

*Recognising and Recording Progress and Achievement* in non-accredited learning, a five-stage process for evidencing learning by adults on programmes that do not lead to a qualification.

**VLE**

*Virtual Learning Environment*. A system, almost always online, for managing learner and teacher access to resources, assignments, etc.

**VoIP**

*Voice over Internet Protocol*. Technology that enables telephone calls to be made over the internet and other computer networks.

# References

Arts Award (undated [1]) *Gold Arts Award*, available at
www.artsaward.org.uk/site/?id=67 (accessed 12 February 2014).

Arts Award (undated [2]) *What is Arts Award?*, available at
www.artsaward.org.uk/site/?id=1346 (accessed 12 February 2014).

Burgess, B. (2012) 'The higher education achievement report: reforming degree
classifications', *Guardian Higher Education Network Blog*, available at
www.theguardian.com/higher-education-network/blog/2012/oct/03/higher-
education-achievement-report-bob-burgess (accessed 12 February 2014).

Cain, S. (2012) *Quiet: The Power of Introverts in a World That Can't Stop Talking*,
London: Viking.

Churchill, W. (1930) *My Early Life,* London: Thornton Butterworth.

Dashwood, M.C. (2014) quoted in Buchan, K. (2014) 'Our expert filters out the very
best', *The Observer,* 9 February 2014, available at
www.theguardian.com/technology/2014/feb/07/best-coffee-makers-tried-and-tested-
barista (accessed 12 February 2014).

Demos (2005) *About Learning: Report of the Learning Working Group,* available at
www.demos.co.uk/files/About_learning.pdf?1240939425 (accessed 12 February
2014).

De Pree, M. (1989) *Leadership Is An Art*. New York: Doubleday.

Garnett, F. (2011a) *WikiQuals: Participatory Learning for Participatory Democracy,*
available at http://wikiquals.wordpress.com/about/ (accessed 12 February 2014).

Garnett, F. (2011b) *WikiQuals Accreditation,* available at
http://wikiquals.wordpress.com/2011/12/19/wikiquals-accreditation/ (accessed 12
February 2014).

Gould, J. and Day, P. 'Hearing you loud and clear: student perspectives of audio
feedback in higher education' in *Assessment & Evaluation in Higher Education,* 38 (5).
London: Routledge.

HEAR (2014) *Higher Education Achievement Report home page,* available at
www.hear.ac.uk/ (accessed 12 February 2014).

Higher Education Academy Engineering Subject Centre (2011) *Deep and Surface Approaches to Learning*, available at http://exchange.ac.uk/learning-and-teaching-theory-guide/deep-and-surface-approaches-learning.html (accessed 12 February 2014).

Illich, I. (1971) *Deschooling Society,* available at http://ournature.org/~novembre/illich/1970_deschooling.html#chapter6 (accessed 12 February 2014).

Jisc (2013a) *Plagiarism programme,* available at www.jisc.ac.uk/whatwedo/programmes/plagiarism.aspx (accessed 12 February 2014).

Jisc (2013b) *So what are Open Badges?*, available at www.jisc.ac.uk/blog/so-what-are-open-badges-28-aug-2013 (accessed 12 February 2014).

Larsson, D. (2012) Tweet available at https://twitter.com/SpiderOak/status/225298327518982144 (accessed 12 February 2014).[7]

Lorenzo, G. and Ittelson, J. (2005) *An Overview of E-Portfolios*, available at http://net.educause.edu/ir/library/pdf/eli3001.pdf (accessed 12 February 2014).

Mozilla Open Badges (undated) *About Mozilla Open Badges*, available at http://openbadges.org/about/ (accessed 12 February 2014).

OCR (2013) *Level 3 - Assessor Qualifications: Centre Handbook,* available at www.ocr.org.uk/Images/68093-level-3-assessor-qualifications-centre-handbook.pdf (accessed 12 February 2014).

QAA (2006) *Code of Practice for the Assurance of Academic Quality and Standards in Higher Education*, available at www.qaa.ac.uk/Publications/InformationAndGuidance/Documents/COP_AOS.pdf (accessed 12 February 2014).

Ravet, S. (2013) *Punished by Open Badges,* available at www.eportfolio.eu/articles/news/punished-open-badges (accessed 12 February 2014).

---

[7] This tweet appears to be based on a better-known saying of Gabriel García Márquez: 'All human beings have three lives: public, private, and secret.'

Sica, G. (2013) Comment on *Unthinkable? Hooray for Tick-box Culture,* available at www.theguardian.com/commentisfree/2013/may/24/unthinkable-box-ticking-approval (accessed 12 February 2014).

Trinity College London (2014) *Arts Award*, available at www.trinitycollege.co.uk/site/?id=59 (accessed 12 February 2014).

Turner, J. (2012) quotation cited in: Jisc (2012) *Crossing the Threshold: Moving E-portfolios into the Mainstream,* available at www.jisc.ac.uk/media/documents/programmes/elearning/eportfolios/threshold.pdf (accessed 12 February 2014).

# Notes

# Notes

# Notes